Broken But Perfect

A phase we all went through

Magesh.K

BookLeaf Publishing

India | USA | UK

Made with ❤ on the BookLeaf Publishing Platform
www.bookleafpub.in
www.bookleafpub.com

Dedication

"Dedicated to my mom and my brother —thank you for always being there.
For my moon, stars, and universe—thank you for your light."

Preface

If you're reading this, then perhaps there is—or was—a moon in your life too. A moon you cherished, adored, and loved with all your heart, only to watch it disappear one day, shrinking little by little until it was gone.

Don't worry... you're not alone. This is a phase many of us have endured, a sorrow shared by countless hearts. But if I were to promise that reading this book would make you forget, or magically move on, I'd be lying. There is no such book.

The pain is real, and moving forward is hard. But through every poem in these pages, from the first to the last, I hope to carry your heavy heart—like a boat floating through the tides of sorrow, grief, and longing. I hope these words connect you to the emotions you've faced, the wounds you've nursed, and the strength you've unknowingly built.

And most of all, I hope this book helps you realize that life does not end with one lost moon. There are other moons, other stars, and a vast sky waiting for you. May this book serve as a rope—but remember, only you can pull yourself up.

So take your time, feel every word, and when you're ready—rise.

Acknowledgements

Writing this book has been a journey—one that I could not have completed alone.

To my family, thank you for your patience, love, and unwavering belief in me, even when I doubted myself. Your support has been my foundation.

To my mentors, senior colleagues, and brothers— Ramanan anna and Darshan anna—thank you for listening to my endless ramblings, reading my early drafts, and encouraging me when I needed it the most. A special thanks to my favorite senior colleague, Shrish anna, who not only believed in me but also pushed me to bring this book to life.

To that one friend from college—the biggest fan and sharpest critic of my writing—your frank, constructive feedback has shaped me into a better writer. Thank you for always being honest and for making me strive for more.

To the moon that once shined in my life—you may be gone, but the memories you left behind have found a home in these pages.

And to you, dear reader—thank you for picking up this book. These poems now belong to you.

1. Broken

*There is no soul, just blood and
bones;
She took it all as if she owns.
She has much love, but not for
me—
My poor heart wished that it
could be.*

*Pain drizzled from my eyes
As she broke all my ties.
I hope she knows, each day I
crumble;
The pain I bear is ineffable.*

The little she spoke pierced my heart,
Yet this wounded heart still wants her back.

2. A Poem Without Love

*The day he heard someone's
heart,
The smile turned genuine;
Words never spoken from the
mouth,
But emotions were teleported
within.*

*Her eyes became his guiding
light,
Routine bent to love's delight.
Life played like a perfect song—
Until, suddenly, it all went
wrong.*

*A shattering sound, a world
undone,
Pain replaced the warming sun.*

*He wakes, the nightmare fades
away,
And as the dawn brings in the
day,
He learns that life still holds its
tune—
A poem complete, with or
without love's boon.*

All he needs is himself.

3. A Ray of light

Day by day i am going down;
With a little bit of hope to be
back on.
Darkest days are getting even
gloomy,
Just need a ray of light to fill my
heart.

Is there a path to start anew,
Or is my dream a fading view?
Chasing echoes of my past,
Wondering if this pain will last.

I pray these lost days drift away,
Before I'm just a name that fades.
I longed to lead, to stand up tall,
But here I am—an outcast, small.

Yet time moves on—both pain
and past,
No storm nor sorrow ever lasts.
So I endure when the skies are
gray
As every night will turn into a
bright day

4. Her Happiness

*I was her choice, but never the
chosen one.
I was a maybe, while he was the
one.
I might have been her desire, but
he was her love.
I had a place in her life, but she
was my world.*

*The moment of truth was
shaking,
Yet my heart is still aching.
I can't do anything about it,
Though I try hard to sleep on it.*

Had I known her love, I would have been a spectator,
A quiet spectator, watching love unfold.
Grateful that it was my heart that broke, not hers.
May she always find happiness.

5. Hope

I was just born,
Yet the days are gone.
My purse is torn,
She was long gone.

Still, I stand,
Without a band.
The world shines twelve hours
bright,
But my life feels like night.

Life is never in line,
Yet I refuse to whine.

Even if I don't shine,
I won't resign.

At the end of the rope,
Struggling to cope,
Still, I live on hope.

I will build a legacy,
While others chase fantasy.
Success begins to resonate,
I am passionate.

I will strive till my last breath,
Hope will stay with me till death.

6. A Cosmic Tragedy

*The moon looks surreal and
lovely,
Longing to be loved by the flower
fairly.
But the flower blooms only for
the sun,
Not because the moon is an
unworthy one—
It simply shows the flower's love
and loyalty.*

*The flower whispers, "You're
beautiful,"
Not out of love, but to make the*

moon stay,
So she can rest beneath his gentle
light.
Yet when morning comes, the
bees weep for the moon,
For he knows nothing of what
happens in the day—
And still, he returns with love
once again.

7. Happily Broken

The hardest thing is seeing her
Hold someone else's hand before
my eyes.
Does it make me cry?
No—at least someone confessed
their love to her.
But it does break my heart.

Crying without tears,
Trying, knowing I'll never have
her.
All I want is to see her happy,
So I remain happily broken.

8. Adieu

*We boarded the train, a
destination in mind,
Yet the journey itself was one of
a kind.
Through laughter and lessons, we
lost track of time,
And now that it's ending, the
climb feels sublime.*

*Each morning, the alarm was a
battle to fight,
Now I long for its ring to wake
me in light.
For today is the day that I bid my*

goodbyes,
With memories painted in tear-
brimmed eyes.

To friends I have known and
those I have missed,
Each moment we shared will
always exist.
The classroom that echoed with
whispers and cheer,
May never again hold us all near.

But life is a journey, not just a
stay,
Paths will cross in some future

day.
The clock strikes now—my final
bell rings,
One last run, as my heart still
clings.

9. Let go...

I gave you my love,
Lent you my heart to call your
own.
Hoped to be cherished, but
instead, I shattered,
Never thought you'd hand what
was mine to another.

Crumbling, crippling, screaming
in pain,
Drowning in sorrow, yet silence
remains.
I long to move on from what felt
like forever,

But love doesn't fade—it lingers,
untethered.

Chaos within has made me
serene,
I've chosen to let go, to wipe my
mind clean.
Yet in the quiet, one truth still
stands—
I stopped thinking of you, but
love never ends.

10. Storm

Every night, I cry,
Refusing to let my love die.
I will put up a fight,
Even though I know it's not
right.

I tried fighting against the tide,
Yet my efforts washed aside.
She was the moon, distant and
bright,
A dream forever out of sight.

I weakened when truth took hold

—

She was a storm, fierce yet cold.
She came, she struck, she tore me apart,
Then left—silence drowning my heart.

Now, my heart is empty.

11. The Aftermath

It was plain pain and calm after the storm had passed.
I tried to close the door, breaking my wrist fast.
Still, the storm tore apart my lovely nest,
I drowned, though I wore a safety vest.

Yet, I didn't die—that was the twist,
Fighting for happiness with my own fist.
Now is the time for no rest,

I rose and stood tall,
Hoping to mend my mental wall.

Pulling back from where I fell,
I saw the sun, bright and well.
Feeling fresh after pain so rainy,
Relieved that it had left, finally.
Now, I try to build hope from
scratch,
Reclaiming all that life had
snatched.

12. Unshakable

People may doubt,
They may call me fake,
But their words are not mine to take.
Nothing will make me shake.

Money is what I strive to make,
It's time for me to wake.
Rushing forward, no hitting the brakes,
There's nothing here at stake.

I won't do this for namesake,

*Even when my whole body
aches.
Haters stay wide awake,
I'll give them all a headache.*

*Hard work is my intake,
Success will be my cheesecake.
Pushing me is a big mistake.
Winning isn't a piece of cake,
Still success is mine to undertake.*

13. The Flight of Fire

It takes years to become a bee,
Yet people push us to sting like
one in a day.
But I am a bee that doesn't sting
—I sing.

Bees weren't built to fly,
Yet they never stop to question
why.
My peers sip nectar from flowers,
But I chase the fire in the sky.

Reaching for it may kill me,

But what truly kills me is never
trying.
There are no rules for me to
follow, so I break them.
No principles to bind me—so
don't preach them.

For that one day, I live my day
one.
There will be no co-achievers—
only me.
Haters will understand when it's
done.
Yes, I will burn when I touch the
sun,

But I will never run.

27

I will win—whether I succeed or die trying.

14. Rising for Her

A well-mannered boy, so kind
and true,
In many hearts, his warmth grew.
Through struggles deep, he never
told,
Yet every fall made him bold.

He pushes hard, beyond his limit,
Sweat and blood—his every
minute.
All for a future yet to be,
Inspired by the one who set him
free.

She shaped the man he's come to
be,
Now he helps all those he sees.
He'll fight until his last breath's
due,
For the one who gave him life so
true.

He's ready to give his all,
For the woman who caught his
fall.
No matter how deep, he'll rise
again,
Just to see her smile through the
pain.

His mother, his guide, his light so
bright,
Wishing only for his joy in sight.
Once, he chased a distant moon,
But now, he's rising—coming
home soon.

15. Happily Broken

I love to see her loved so right,
To see her smile, to see her
bright.
It doesn't matter if I'm pushed
away,
She's all that matters—my love
will stay.

Even if my heart is torn,
I cherish the love that I have
borne.
Love may hurt, it cuts so deep,
But it's a pain I choose to keep.

Heartbreak is hard, but I won't run,
Better to love than to have none.
Life is big, and now I see,
Moving on has set me free.

Yet my eyes will always tell,
A love that time could never quell.
Even when I'm old and gray,
I'll love her just the same way.

Happily broken, but never apart,
Loving her still—with all my heart.

16. Fearless Rise

*God makes me long for what's
not mine,
A distant dream, a fading sign.
I reach, I ache, yet slip away,
Hope dissolves like mist in day.*

*Where I would be, whom I would
hold,
The life I crave, the dreams
untold.
Yet here I stand, lost in the tide,
With a broken heart, yet arms
open wide.*

*I mend the cracks that cannot
heal,
Chasing ghosts I barely feel.
Control eludes, fate takes the
lead,
So I surrender, let it feed.*

*Let the universe carve my way,
Through night's despair and
weary day.
Heartbreak merely carves my
soul,
A lesson learned to make me
whole.*

The world is rough, its edges sharp,
Yet I stand strong, embrace the dark.
A warrior forged in fire's embrace,
With fearless heart and steady grace.

Failures come—I do not bow,
Watch me rise, watch me now.
Bring the storm, I'll face its rage,
Smile unfazed, I'll own the stage.

17. From Emptiness to Passion

On this vast, wide world,
Life is beautiful—yet no one told.
Try living it happy and alone;
Friends and family don't have a
role.

Nothing is ever in your control,
All feelings are mere deception.
Let them come and let them go,
One at a time—take it slow.

It's time to put on a show,
From being haunted by

emptiness
To becoming a soul possessed by
passion.

Life is not a game of dice—
Don't just sit and wait for luck.
Move on, move forward,
You won't be left out like a
sitting duck.

I'm here to get my boxes ticked,
So watch me rise—
Here I come.

18. Crowing Your Destiny

You can be the king—so don't choose to beg.
You can be the greatest—so don't settle for less.
You can be the best—so never stop short.
You can conquer the world—so don't rest too soon.
You can win this war—so start the hustle.

Let it go.

Holding her today may be easy,
But she may make your
tomorrow hard.
Letting her go today may be
painful,
But it will bring you peace
tomorrow.

Be your own idol—get inspired.
Strive for success, chase your
dreams,
And let your journey become
The most inspirational story the
world has ever seen.

19. Life Begins and Ends with Love

Life begins with love and ends the same way.
I was born crying, embraced by love,
Yet as I live, love feels distant—
No one will truly love me until the day I don't wake up.

No matter how much I love or care,
I remain an option, never a priority.
She will never find a heart that

loves her more than mine,
Yet she moved on with ease,
Discarding me as if I were
nothing.

I wait, I hope, I pretend it doesn't
hurt,
But deep inside, it aches—
She never feared losing me.
Even when no one else does, she
let me go.

But someday, someone will
choose me first—
Not as a backup, not as a

convenience,
But as their one and only.
Until then, I will choose myself,
Love myself, and stand tall.

Because in the end, I will be okay
—

And if I'm not, then it's not the
end.
A broken heart doesn't mean life
stops;
She broke my heart to open my
eyes.

One day, a woman will walk into

my life,
And I will love her with all my
heart.
Together, we will grow old,
Proving that life truly ends with
love.

20. From the Moon to My Star

When time flies and a decade passes,
The one I once loved becomes a stranger,
And the stranger I never knew becomes my world.

When I had lost all hope in love,
She became the hope that brought me the love
I thought I would never have again.

*From loving someone to being
truly loved—
It felt surreal.
I pinched myself just to see if it
was real.*

*The love I received kept growing,
And two of us became three.
From loving a woman with all
my heart
To loving my little girl with all
my soul—
Holding her tiny hands felt even
better than holding hers.*

*I once thought there was only
one moon,
But God sent me a star—
One that shines and sings with
love.*

*For the times I thought she never
gave me anything,
Now, I hold the greatest gift in
my arms.
I hope the moon knows that I've
landed on a lovely star,
And I still pray that my moon
lives happily.*

21. Unfinished Verse

*Life didn't end there—it was just
a pause.
It was hard; your friends told you
to let go,
Even your conscience wanted to
close that chapter.*

*You might have loved her more
deeply than you even knew.
Leaving someone you can never
unlove is close to impossible.
Yet, this is the moment you need
to love someone even more—
That someone is you.*

*You deserve all the love you gave
her.
This is the time to show yourself
the love you truly deserve.
Prioritize yourself above all else.
Discover what life feels like
when you love yourself.*

*When you start loving yourself,
One day, the universe will send
you the love meant for you.
That day will come.
But first, you must begin with
yourself.*

So endure the pain today.
And in the end, I never truly let
her go.
Those eyes I can never forget—
She still has a place in my heart.

But the pain is no longer there.
She will forever remain a
memory,
One I will take with me to my
grave.

And finally, if you are reading
this—

"You are the poem I never
wanted to end."